A Geek's Guide to Unicorn Ranching

Advice for Couples Seeking Another Partner

A Geek's Guide
to
Unicorn Ranching

Advice for Couples
Seeking Another Partner

By
Page Turner

Braided Studios, LLC
PO Box 770670
Lakewood, OH 44107
https://braided.studio

Published By: Braided Studios, LLC

ISBN: 978-1-947296-02-2

Thanks to those who read this book early:

Amy

Creston Hetzel

Elan

Kat Rhys

Matt

Susan

Tom

A special thanks to our Patreons

Elan

Jason Daubert

Jeff

Jennifer

Kat Rhys

Sarah

Tom

Cover Art by: Cynthia Lee

Contents

Introduction

If you're reading this book, chances are you've found a great partner and are in a fantastic romantic relationship. You've talked things over and have mutually decided that you'd like to find another person to date together.

Who the Heck Am I and Why Should You Listen to Me?

These are fair questions. You should listen to me because I know quite a bit about being the third partner. I'm a bisexual woman who has dated couples (also known as a unicorn), as well as someone who knows multiple long-term stable and happy triads.

From those experiences, I've learned what differentiates couples who do it well and ones who… well, really should have read this book.

The first time I was intimate with a couple, it was a wonderful experience. In many ways, I preferred the unicorn role to being on the other side of things, when I'd been part of the couple.

When I was a unicorn, I was the guest star. The couple lavished attention on me. Wonderful dinners. Little gifts. Physical affection. As a unicorn, I began to understand what it might be like to be an only child (I have three siblings).

This couple positively spoiled me.

It was carnally exciting to be physical with not one but two new shiny partners.

And their dynamic was sweet. Their bond with one another was strong, stable. They treated each other — and me — with respect.

I was filled inside with my own well of New Relationship Energy, and when we made love, I felt their Old Relationship Energy with each other wash over me like a giant wave. I was the gasoline to their fire.

When conducted ethically, honestly, and respectfully, three-person relationships (also known as triads or occasionally throuples) can be absolutely wonderful. But skimp on any of those elements? You're asking for disaster.

Lesson One

Don't Be a Ferengi

*Bear with me for a hot second because I'm
about to get super geeky.*

"Oh great," my friend says. "Another married couple newly
opened up. How original."

I smile, but uncomfortably. Wondering if my friend judges
me for my past. She's solo poly, long single. And not open to
couples. In fact, she adds, she gets sick even thinking about
dating a couple.

"I know I couldn't get past feeling excluded," she says. "Like I
was less a part of the relationship since I wasn't one of them."

"Well, you know I've dated couples myself," I reply. "And if you
feel that way, it could be that you're not cut out for couples,
sure. But for me, it's always been more a sign I'm dating a shitty
couple."

"I just know myself." She sighs. "So many freaking couples
looking for a third."

Me and hubby are new to poly, the forum post reads. *How do
you go about meeting females who will join your relationship?
We're looking for someone to share our lives with.*

I find that "female" or "females" in its noun form is never a good move. I invariably read it in a Ferengi voice. And I've yet to meet unicorn hunters with the lobes to pull that off.

183 commenters have already let the original poster know every other thing they find troubling or annoying about the post. "Hubby" is such an infantile term, one says. Several others criticize her for "share our lives with." Because it's so good to know she and hubby can tear off a piece of their own life together like a piece of stale bread. A slice of crouton thrown to a starving bisexual babe orphan.

I cringe. For everyone's sake.

> *Geeky Side Note: A Ferengi is a fictional alien race in the Star Trek universe, most prominently featured on The Next Generation and Deep Space Nine. Ferengi society discriminates against women. Ferengi women are not allowed to work, leave their homes on their own, or even wear clothes. And, memorably, a recurring Ferengi main character named Quark emphatically proclaims "Females!" with disdain whenever a woman acts with autonomy. Normally right before he says something extra sexist.*

Lesson Two

When Someone Calls You a Unicorn Hunter

"Oooh, ahhh, that's how it always starts. Then later there's running and screaming."

Ian Malcolm, The Lost World: Jurassic Park

Unicorn hunters get a bum rap in polyamory, despite being very common, especially among poly newbies. Speaking most traditionally, a "unicorn" is a polyamorous, bisexual woman who will date both members of a couple. Occasionally some couples will be looking for a man to date together, although this is less common. The couple that opens up a previously closed relationship and is looking for this unicorn to form a three-person relationship, they're the unicorn hunters. This sounds all fine and good, right?

And it should be.

Except it can be a difficult (even scary) thing to come in as a new person to an already established relationship. For starters, you are literally outnumbered. It's two on one. Not to mention that there's a power imbalance from shared history in this pre-existing relationship. The couple may also have ties from living together, legal protections like marriage, kids, etc.

It certainly doesn't help that many couples place additional restrictions on the unicorn they're dating. This unicorn may be barred from having other partners of their own.

The setup can become especially troublesome if the unicorn is hidden from the couple's extended family but expected to live with them. Whenever anyone the couple isn't out as polyamorous to (family, coworkers, etc.) is over, the unicorn may be expected to hide or act as a maid or babysitter. This can be especially stressful and exclusionary when the holidays come around.

Some couples may even stipulate that the unicorn is required to love both parts of the couple equally — which is arguably not even a thing that's possible to control.

This controlling and imbalanced behavior is common enough that if you're a single poly woman who dates enough couples, you're bound to run into these kinds of unicorn hunters every once in a while.

So while you may have every good intention in the world, the couples who have come before you made a very bad impression. One that you must work extra hard to overcome.

Yes, it's annoying. Yes, it's unfair, but it's reality.

Before you get to your fantasy, you have to deal with reality.

Lesson Three

It's Dangerous to Go Alone, Take This!

Before you add another partner, get your affairs in order.

It's common to hear from couples who are newly opening up and looking for a third partner: "We want to find someone to complete our relationship."

Honey, if your relationship is incomplete before you open, it's going to be incomplete after you open. It's the same relationship.

In fact, many couples find that polyamory exposes issues in their relationship that they were previously unaware of. While "relationship broken, add more people" is a simple recipe, it's also one that rarely produces anything delicious.

Before adding another partner, make sure your core relationship is as strong as it can be. Get your finances in order. If you need couples therapy, go.

Once you've covered those basics, here are a few other things you can do before setting out to make the journey a little less perilous.

Figure Out if You're on the Same Page

Before you set out into the wilds of non-monogamy, take a second to check in with each other. You don't have to have the same answers to these questions, but knowing where your partner is coming from (even if it differs from where you're coming from) can help stave off nasty surprises.

Things to Ask:

- Why do you want to do this?

- What are you hoping to get out of the experience? People have a variety of reasons why they open relationships.

- What values are important to you when it comes to relationships?

- What role do those values play in your current relationship?

- How do you ideally see those values playing out in new relationships? Generally speaking, of course, since new partners will bring their own values as well.

- How actively will you seek out partners?

- Will you make a concerted effort to seek out new relationships through conventional means, maintaining multiple dating profiles, reaching out many times with clear propositions?

- Or will you take a more passive and less direct approach, coming out as poly to people you know, making new friends in poly communities, and seeing if anything develops naturally?

Set a Relationship Agreement

Once you've discussed your motivations, values, and desired approaches to seeking out partners, it's time to come up with a relationship agreement.

Above all else: Be specific, clear, and comprehensive.

As a starting point, here are some questions that have guided developing agreements that I've made in the past:

- How much freedom or autonomy do we need?

- What concerns us regarding sexual safety?

- What painful scenarios have we run into in the past (while monogamous, casually non-monogamous, or polyamorous) that we are we looking to avoid? Are there any measures that we can implement to prevent these?

- Do we want to have a permission structure (i.e., to have a standard that we ask and obtain approval from an existing partner before we start a new relationship) or a notification structure (i.e., don't need permission but should tell our partners things happened after they happen)? Or something else altogether (e.g., don't ask don't tell, etc.)?

- What are the consequences of breaking the relationship agreement?

This is just a beginning. Developing a comprehensive understanding of each other's concerns can be quite a twisty-turny process and lead to all sorts of places that are hard to predict until you get in the thick of things.

So does an agreement need to be the size of a phone book? Not necessarily. They're precisely as long as they need to be in order to get the job done. Sometimes this means the agreements themselves are short. Other times, this means they're lengthy.

If you're unclear about something, ask. If you don't understand what the other person means, about anything, ask them. Many people find it helpful to write their agreement out once it's been decided so they have a reference.

However, as you write up your relationship agreement, please bear in mind that it's very common to find that your relationship agreement works out differently in practice than it did in theory.

When this happens, it's important to check back in and discuss. Even renegotiate the terms. This is especially true when you're brand new to polyamory, and it's your very first relationship agreement. You will almost certainly find that something needs to be tweaked once you've road tested it.

Relationship agreements are very individual. What works for one person might be terrible for another. However, it sometimes helps to see what other people have come up with. Please see Appendix A for sample relationship agreements.

Talk About Exit Strategy

It might sound weird to talk about the end of something at the beginning — but when you set up an agreement is a perfect time to talk about its end.

Here are some questions to help with that:

- How often will you revisit the agreement?

- Is it one and done?

- Do you have an "out clause?"

- Is one party able to unilaterally end things at any one time?

- Do you have veto power over your partner's other relationships? And if you do, what does that look like?

Build in Check-Ins

As you navigate unfamiliar territory, it's invaluable to check back in and discuss what's going on. As you're setting out, make a commitment to check-ins. These are great for processing *and* for making sure that you're setting enough time aside for reconnecting with one another.

Your ideal check-in setup will likely revolve around your schedules and how complicated (or uncomplicated) your love lives are. And how much you're comfortable sharing and when.

As one example, a partner and I had the wine pledge. At the time we opened up, we had a subscription box that brought us four bottles of wine every month. We made the commitment to drink those four bottles together. If we simply couldn't make that time for one another, we'd know we were doing something wrong and that it needed to change.

Plus, we had a tendency to try to "out-nice" each other a bit, and in our consideration for one another's feelings, we could tiptoe around issues to the point where nothing gets said.

Wine had a twofold purpose here — first, it turned us both into Stage 5 blurters so that the truth was even spoken, and second, it dulled the sting of whatever unpleasant thing was said.

It Helps If You Have Polyamorous Friends

When I first tried polyamory many years ago, it was because I discovered friends of mine had been discreetly polyamorous for a couple of years. Before them, I'd never even heard the word.

I was *really* lucky in a lot of ways. It was invaluable to watch those friends and learn and discuss things through them.

It really helps to have polyamorous friends — a bit like watching videos of a driver going around a racetrack before you attempt it yourself.

However, if you don't have real-life poly friends, don't sweat it. The Internet isn't a bad place either to observe poly dynamics, although it can be tough sometimes to know how accurate the stories of online posters are. What they are sharing with others could radically diverge from their lived experience.

If you can, find a local poly group (Meetup.com and Fetlife.com have many) that meets in person and make some friends there.

Get Tested for STIs and Read Up on Sexual Health

Make an appointment to get tested for STIs. You can go to your regular healthcare provider if you want, but I've had great success with Planned Parenthood. They are *really* non-monogamy friendly.

Read up on sexual health issues and safer sex measures. Don't just read one thing. Read *a lot*. Trust me, it's better to get educated on this stuff *before* you're in complicated situations than trying to figure it out as you go along.

Believe it or not, PornHub has great resources. Scarleteen is also brilliant.

Since you're new to ethical non-monogamy, you might feel a bit overwhelmed. The good news is that many other couples have been in your shoes.

While you're going to have your own sets of needs and concerns, many couples worry about similar things. Some of these include:

- Discretion about your unconventional relationship model. Not wanting friends, family, coworkers and/or community members to judge your choices or discriminate against you.

- How to "pick" the right person to have a relationship with.

- How to be honest and fair with the new partner.

- Ways to prevent, mitigate, and/or manage jealousy.

- Protecting the existing relationship.

In the next few lessons, we'll discuss common pitfalls that couples face when addressing these.

Lesson Four

Discreet as Fuck. Keep it Secret, Keep it Safe

"Discretion is the better part of valor."

William Shakespeare

It's a big shift to go from a monogamous way of thinking to considering non-monogamous alternatives. Polyamory and other forms of ethical non-monogamy aren't modeled for us that often in broader culture.

Worse yet, many people shame or disparage non-monogamous people. If you're like most people, there was some soul-searching involved, and you may have had to deal with your own inner doubts.

It's understandable, given all of this, that you aren't eager to open yourself up to external criticism. The last thing you probably want is a lecture from people close to you, or in some cases, to lose friends or family entirely.

Couples with children also face the additional worry about how polyamory will affect custody decisions, although it's encouraging to note that recent trends show more legal acceptance for non-monogamy in custody cases (for example,

Dawn M. v. Michael M., 2017[1]).

In the court of public opinion, however, polyamory isn't on equal footing with monogamy.

Because of these factors, many couples make being discreet about their lifestyle a priority.

As individuals we absolutely have the choice to value and protect our own privacy. However, there's a flipside to this as well. We also absolutely have the choice to be open about our lives.

Think about your relationship status on social media. Most long-term couples add it to their Facebook profiles ("in a relationship with," "married to," etc.).

Sure, it's informational. But to many? This type of social relationship signaling is a source of pride.

I can't tell you how many times I've had a single friend gleefully tell me they were about to make a relationship "Facebook official."

When you closet yourself as polyamorous, you also closet the third partner.

This can work for some people – but others? Not so much.

Because you are able to broadcast your existing relationship to the world at large, the burden suffered by the third partner is greater. They can't share the fact that they're in a wonderful, loving relationship widely with others, and if it gets bad enough, they may start to feel shame, like they're a "dirty secret."

It can become especially difficult to hide from others if the relationship becomes serious, and the third person moves in. The holidays can be particularly trying. What used to be a fun holiday with friends and family can make the third partner feel excluded when they're not allowed to attend.

If family comes to visit, it can be difficult and stressful. Being displaced in a hotel is inconvenient and expensive (and again, makes them feel excluded). Pretending they're a housekeeper or nanny isn't any better since it's stressful and reinforces shame and feelings of exclusion.

What I've seen work well with couples in the past is a middle path approach: Being relatively low key and quiet about polyamory until a triad becomes serious and then opening up to people who are likely to discover it – y'know, the people you would have to lie to or hide things from.

All things considered, the more open you can afford to be about it, the better. Not only is it less stress on the third partner, but you'll find it much easier to find relationships in the first place if you're out. (More on that later in Lesson Nine).

Lesson Five

Eeny, Meeny, Miney Moe: Partner Selection and Expectation Management

*"When you stop expecting people to be perfect,
you can like them for who they are."*

Donald Miller

Deciding exactly what you want out of other people before you actually meet them?

It's a bit like getting your heart set on what you're going to build before you see which LEGO blocks are actually in the box.

I'm not saying that you can't luck out and stumble onto a dream partner exactly like you envisioned (and have them like you back, just like that), but it's certainly not guaranteed. Besides, sometimes we discover people who are nothing like we would have expected to encounter but are amazing anyway.

You know the trope of the woman with the extremely long checklist for Mr. Right? Of course you do. You also know what happens to her: She bemoans her fate over cocktails with her similarly miserable friends.

Don't let this happen to you. Forget about *Sex and the City*. Few couples look great gallivanting around Manhattan in Manolo Blahniks (although if you can pull this off, don't let *me* stop you).

So instead of coming up with a long list of "must haves" and "immediate disqualifiers," focus on the ones that are most important to you.

Yours of course will vary depending on your values, but here are some traits that are commonly cited as requirements:

- Sense of humor

- Good communication skills

- Emotional stability

- Kindness

- Honesty

As you develop a list of things you look for in a partner, ask yourselves:

- How do we size up to this list (together *and* individually)?

- Are we asking more of a partner than we are willing or able to provide?

When forming expectations, stay away from dictating a future partner's behavior or emotional states. For example, avoid statements like, "Our ideal partner will love us both equally," or "Our ideal partner will date us and us alone."

These are descriptions of potential relationship dynamics (equal love) and structures (dating only you, a.k.a., polyfidelity, more on that later). Relationship dynamics and structures are not actually related to a person's personality traits. You can put two people very similar in personality into the same situation, and they will react differently and feel and need different things.

The "You Will Love Us Both Equally" Fallacy

It's difficult, verging on impossible, to force yourself to love two people equally. Anyone who has dated couples can attest to this.

Sometimes it happens that way naturally. Sometimes it doesn't. I've additionally been in situations where I am terribly fond of both halves of a couple, but in different ways.

It's honestly kind of weird to quantify and compare love to see if it's "equal." Emotions are funny. It's not like currency, where you can say, "This love dollar splits nicely into four love quarters."

So by making "loving us both equally" a requirement for the relationship, you are setting the third partner up to fail.

Lesson Six

The Wonderful World of Three-Person Relationship Structures

"It seems to me that the best relationships, the ones that last, are frequently the ones that are rooted in friendship."

Dana Skully, The X-Files

Part of keeping an open mind is also understanding that there is no one standard configuration for a three-person relationship. Many common configurations exist.

They vary by unanimous or partial romantic involvement (triad vs. vee), being closed or open to new partners (polyfidelity vs. open polyamory), and whether or not there's a pecking order (hierarchical vs. non-hierarchical). Hierarchical poly can further be broken down into descriptive vs. prescriptive hierarchy.

Whew, that's a mouthful. I'll explain.

Triads Vs. Vees

If you're reading this book, you are (probably) in a couple. Another word for a couple is a *dyad*, or a group of two people. A group of three people is called a *triad*. (And less commonly, a throuple.)

In polyamory, a triad is most commonly used to mean a group of three people who are all romantically involved with each other in some way.

Where in a dyad there is only one relationship (Alex & Baley), in a triad there are actually at least *three* separate relationships:

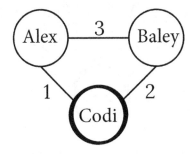

1. Alex and Codi

2. Baley and Codi

3. Alex and Baley

Some would argue that a fourth relationship exists, the group dynamic of all partners when they are together.

Many couples enter polyamory looking to form a triad. However, another three-person configuration exists and is quite common. This configuration is called a *vee*, much like the letter V.

In a vee, two of the partners are linked by a relationship in common, and this linking person is called the *hinge*. And the two people within the vee who aren't the hinge have no romantic relationship with one another.

Here is an example of a vee, with Codi as the hinge:

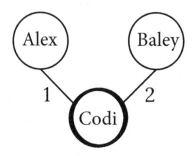

1. Alex and Codi

2. Baley and Codi

Polyfidelity Vs. Open Polyamory

Another important factor is whether or not the relationship is open to new partners.

As the name would suggest, in open polyamory, all relationships are typically open. If you formed a triad or a vee with a third partner, they would still be permitted to date others and take on new romantic and/or sexual partners. And so would you.

Conversely, polyfidelity is a style where multiple people are all exclusively committed to one another. If you were in a polyfidelitous triad, it would be different from monogamy in that everyone involved would have multiple partners (in this case, two partners apiece), but it would be similar to monogamy in that no one would be permitted to date new people outside of the triad.

It's important to note that some relationships even fall somewhere in between these two styles.

For example, you might find that the person you form a triad with is married to someone else (who you aren't involved with but knows of and approves of their spouse dating you). The three of you then might mutually agree that there will be no additional *new* partners, aside from the preexisting relationship your partner already has with their spouse.

Or you might find that being closed to partners temporarily works, with the understanding that you will be open later. I often find this situation with newer relationships, where members want to strengthen a bond and make sure they have the hang of their current dynamics before introducing too many variables into the equation (so to speak). Unit testing, or at least beta testing.

Polyamorous people sometimes war among themselves regarding what the "best" way is to do things.

Like many things, whether you choose polyfidelity or open polyamory all depends on what makes the sense for all three of you, and so long as you mutually agree on terms, it's all ethical.

Because of this, I would recommend keeping an open mind and not getting your heart set on one over the other until you actually meet the person (or people) you're going to date since you will be involving their needs and wants in the decision-making process. Because if you don't include their priorities, then it's a recipe for disaster. Plus, individual personalities and situations can shape what works for a triad or vee (for example, whether people are introverted or extroverted, how much free time they have, etc.).

Hierarchical Vs. Non-Hierarchical

Relationships also differ based on whether there's a hierarchy.

In hierarchical polyamory, certain relationships are considered higher priority than others. This is usually noted by calling some relationships "primary" and others "secondary."

Most commonly, primary relationships are ones where partners live together, share resources, make important decisions together, and spend the majority of their time with one another.

Secondary partners, sometimes also known as secondaries, often have less access to time and resources and are usually afforded less of an input into decisions that their partner makes with their primary.

In some cases, people even have relationships they call "tertiary," which usually involve very infrequent contact and are more limited in scope.

Conversely, in non-hierarchical poly, no relationship is ranked or put before the other. There are no primaries or secondaries (or tertiaries). Just relationships. Everyone's inputs and needs are considered.

Descriptive Hierarchy Vs. Prescriptive Hierarchy

"But, Page," you might be saying. "How can I even *have* a non-hierarchical triad? I've been with my existing partner for a while now. We have shared history. We live together. Share finances. Share toothbrushes. How is a new person going to show up and instantly be at that level?"

Well, I'm glad you asked (even if you didn't).

Hierarchy gets a bad rap in poly circles. This is because sometimes couples who are primarily partnered will use it in a way that makes the third partner feel excluded or constantly outnumbered (and outvoted) when they form a new triad.

"Our marriage comes first!" can be really scary and offputting to a third partner, especially if that sentiment is expressed as something that will *always* be that way. Imagine, devoting your whole life to loving someone who you felt could easily put you on the back burner – even discard you! – at a moment's notice.

I call this attitude *prescriptive hierarchy*. In this style, people dictate that one relationship is more important than the other and always will be. This can work sometimes – but usually in situations where the triad is open and the third partner has other relationships, and especially a primary relationship of their own, outside of the triad.

This style is different than *descriptive hierarchy*. In a descriptive hierarchy, yes, you can say that your preexisting partner is a primary relationship but only as a way of describing the current status of higher entanglement (that maybe you live together, raise kids, share finances, etc.).

When you are descriptive about hierarchy, you're not dictating what the future dynamics will be, you are only *describing* the current state of them, and you are open to the possibility of those dynamics changing.

And yes, you can have two primaries! Some polyamorous people have more.

Prescriptive Hierarchy, Incorporated

After a long and exhaustive search chasing dead ends, you finally land a new job that you're excited about.

The company culture is fantastic. The benefits are great. It even pays pretty well… except, well, it's entry level. You're in the right field, but it's not what you dream of doing.

No problem, these things take time. You figure you'll work hard, build up a reputation, and eventually all of your hard work will be rewarded.

At your 90-day review, your supervisor glows about your performance so far. You take the opportunity to let her know your ambitions. What you'd like to see unfold in your career.

"Uhhh… about that," your supervisor says. "I wouldn't get your hopes up too much."

"What do you mean?"

She leans forward on her elbows, lowering her voice. "This isn't exactly a place with a lot of upward mobility."

"Well, how did you get you get promoted?"

"I didn't," she says. "I'm one of the founders."

"But people leave, don't they? Surely spots open up from time to time."

"They haven't yet," she says. "Now, don't get me wrong. I appreciate your ambition. I just want to make sure you have realistic expectations."

After your meeting, you slink back to your desk, disheartened. An office neighbor approaches you. "I couldn't help but overhear. Nice try. But management positions just don't open up here. No one leaves, and they don't let anyone go either."

"No one's ever gotten fired?"

"Not management," your coworker says. "Entry level, sure. If a manager doesn't like you, you're gone. But a manager? They can get away with basically anything. They're untouchable. Their needs always come first."

You're faced with an uncomfortable decision: Do you stick it out here hoping that a rare opportunity will present itself, happy that you've at least found a job and one in your field? Or do you roll the dice on another company that might actually offer you a path to promotion?

✎

Relationship Escalator - A widely held cultural belief about relationships that they must follow a particular pattern, leading to progressively more serious commitment

It's in prescriptive hierarchies that I've really seen secondary partners suffer and struggle the most.

Now, some secondary partners don't mind it all. After all, some folks prefer having lower-entanglement relationships and not every connection needs to become progressively serious (à la the relationship escalator). Just like how there are plenty of people who would rather stick with the job they have because they enjoy it more than they would taking on a bunch of stress being a manager. And to take the analogy further, there are people who moonlight. People with side hustles. Ones who freelance.

However, there are many other people who are like the eager job seeker I just described. Folks who begin a secondary relationship hoping that it will one day become a high-entanglement primary one.

Sometimes it works out. The compatibility is there. A new love that starts out secondary blossoms into a high-entanglement relationship. An anchor partner and/or co-primary.

But other times? Even if compatibility is great, there's no path to promotion.

Lesson Seven

Trusting Your Relationships, Old and New

" I love you."
"I know."

Han and Leia, Return of the Jedi

I'm asking you to take a leap of faith. To be bold and to trust your relationship – and each other.

Because the truth is that no relationship is 100% safe, open or closed. However, instead of accepting this fact, a lot of times people act up in outrageous and unproductive ways.

They check your phone whenever you leave it lying around. "Who's this?" they want to know. "And why did they text you a smiley in the middle of the night?"

They bristle when the waitstaff smiles at you. "Don't think I didn't see that!"

"See what? They were just being friendly."

"Oh, they were being *friendly* all right."

The standard portrait of a jealous partner is one always on the alert, ready to defend from threats from the outside.

Sadly, this doesn't ensure anything. Instead, these attempts backfire.

The way to protect a relationship is *not* to defend it by attacking outside threats – but to build up what you have on the inside.

Once you realize this and truly believe this, you'll realize that bringing in another relationship isn't an outside threat, but instead something that falls under the category of having the potential to strengthen what you already have.

Sometimes people look at love and sex like they're the glue that holds a romantic relationship together and that other people being intimate with us -- emotionally, physically, or both – can cause that bond to become "unglued."

Sure, that vulnerable kind of sex where you're really connected? It can certainly feel like glue. Bind you together. The way that all intimacy does. However, it's not just sex. Shared secrets go a long way. Mutual quirks. Unwavering support that humbles you. It all counts.

There are many kinds of "glue" that hold a relationship together.

Plus, the other nice thing about glue is that adding more glue from another source, like another lover or a friend, doesn't damage the existing connection, provided that no one violently pulls away.

Polyamory's a lot like that. So long as a strong base of trust is there, the collateral attachment can actually *reinforce* what you have. Make that bond even stronger.

This is not to say that adding another partner fixes relationships that are broken or fractured. As I said in Lesson Three, that doesn't work.

However, attachment from another person doesn't have to threaten preexisting attachment and can instead supplement it – potentially even reinforce it – quite beautifully.

Lesson Eight

How to Meet Polyamorous People

"I am looking for someone to share in an adventure."
Gandalf

So you've gotten your affairs in order. Your relationship is solid. Your life is pretty logistically sound. You have a rough idea of what you're looking for, and you've done the mental and emotional preparation necessary to begin exploring polyamory.

You're excited to get started.

The next question is: How do you meet partners? How do you find polyamorous people?

A lot of people hop on a traditional dating platform, like OkCupid or Tinder, and start browsing profiles or swiping. While traditional dating sites can work, there are a couple of other channels that are underutilized by most newly polyamorous couples and frequently lead to much better success rates.

The first of these is finding poly meetups in your area. To do this, you can visit Meetup.com and search for polyamory groups near you. Or you can simply do an internet search for "poly meetup" and your area.

These discussion groups are even better than online dating because they have multiple benefits. Clearly, you can meet new partners through them, but you also get to learn from others and have access to support and help with any difficulty you might have adjusting to polyamory.

Plus, as you make more friends who are polyamorous, even if you don't hit it off romantically with any of them, you grow your network of poly folks you know. The first couple I dated seriously were friends of a poly friend.

Another great option for meeting more polyamorous folks is considering exploring your local kink scene, especially if you're kinky yourself. Not all poly people are kinky of course, but there are a high number of poly people on the kink scene. If you're not sure where to start you can go to Fetlife.com (it's basically Facebook for kinksters) and see if there are any groups in your area (there are many). Search for "polyamory" and your area.

Be sure to read the group rules. Most of these don't allow for personal ads of any kind (though there are a few specialized ones for that purpose, one that springs to mind, active as I write this, "Poly, Kinky & Looking"), but even the ones that don't allow ads can build your knowledge about polyamory and answer your questions and provide an opportunity to meet other like-minded folks, typically with discussion group meetings at coffeehouses or restaurants.

Something to keep in mind: Many people who have been polyamorous for any length of time are used to being hit on or sexualized by people who assume that being poly means that you'll automatically sleep with anyone (which is sooooo not the case). Focus primarily on building friendships with them and getting to know them, and if true compatibility is there, the relationships will follow.

You may also find that people are reluctant to date you at first, if you're newly poly. This is because many outsiders who are new to polyamory don't take the time and care to prepare like you (hopefully) have, and they're watching you to make sure you're not like that. What's interesting is that once you build up a reputation of trustworthiness in a poly circle, and especially once you've dated one person successfully (and have been seen to have treated them ethically), you may very well find the floodgates open. Where once you had a world of hurt getting one date, you may find yourself becoming a hot commodity.

So understand up front that it may be a while before you're successful but that building a reputation is worth it.

Whatever you do, don't ruin your reputation by being too pushy and too eager before people have a chance to get to know you.

What If You're Only Looking for a Physical Relationship?

The focus of this book has been addressing the needs of couples who are looking to have close romantic relationships with others. However, some couples are focused primarily on casual threesomes and purely physical arrangements.

Speaking frankly, partners who are open to hooking up with a couple on a regular basis with "no strings attached" are extremely rare and even more difficult to find. And even so, there typically has to be some other kind of emotional or social connection in place – at the very least a friendship.

That said, I *have* seen occasional arrangements like these in my poly circles. Not with couples who are brand new to polyamory, mind you, but with couples who have had poly friends for a long time, after the casual unicorn friend has had an opportunity to get to know them and fully trust that:

- The couple has the emotional awareness and skillset to manage any potential jealousy and insecurity in a way that won't cause damage to the existing friendship or the couple's relationship.

- The unicorn will be treated with respect by the couple after those casual encounters.

- The couple seems generally honest, ethical, and good at communication.

The reality is that even in seeking out a purely physical relationship, you're much more likely to meet with success in those efforts if you work on the skills that you would need to conduct a romantic relationship.

Essentially, developing a good reputation and working on the skills outlined in this book will matter even *more* if casual hookups are your goal.

Lesson Nine

The High-Success (Though Scariest) Method

"Live now; make now always the most precious time. Now will never come again."
Jean-Luc Picard

While you may have one ideal picture of triad-dom, the more rigid you are in your expectations, the less likely you are to meet someone who ticks all your boxes. Conversely, the more flexible you can be about what you're looking for, the higher likelihood you'll meet with success.

Here are a couple of alternatives to consider in your quest to find another partner that aren't your "typical unicorn scenario" but have led many other people in your shoes to wonderful relationships.

- Consider Dating a Person Who Has Other Partners

- Consider a Square

- Date on Your Own Instead of Dating as a Unit

- Don't Bait and Switch

- Wearing the Friend Hat

- The Good Roommate Standard

Consider Dating a Person Who Has Other Partners

One simple way to improve your chances is to consider dating a person who also has other partners of their own.

Most frequently newly polyamorous couples will want to form a closed polyfidelitous triad with a woman who has no other partners. While this is an attractively tidy and convenient arrangement for many couples, the reality is that there aren't that many unpartnered bisexual women who are looking to date a couple (and only that couple). They do exist, but they're few and far between. Plus, the ones that *are* out there are inundated with offers from other couples looking for the same thing.

However, when you consider bisexual polyamorous women who have partners that are also open to dating couples (provided they're cool), the number goes way up. Additionally, if the person you date already has a primary relationship, they're less likely to care about being secondary (although some still will). So a hierarchical style of polyamory will probably be less of an issue if your third partner is seeing others and has entanglements of their own.

True, you'll have to split time with their other partners and manage any jealousy or insecurity that results from potentially being secondary to their other partners, but fair's fair. As a bonus, it'll give you a better appreciation of how hierarchy can feel when you're secondary, which will help you treat secondary partners more kindly and compassionately.

Consider a Square

It's a well-known fact that the number of couples looking to date a third partner together is much higher than the number of single folks running around looking to date couples. But you know what there is an equal number of?

That's right. Couples.

(By definition, actually. Number of couples = number of couples. Reflexive property for the win! Finally all that *Square One* came in handy. Yay mathifications!).

As you recall, there are a couple different major configurations for relationships that involve three people (i.e., triads vs. vees). As one might expect, there are even *more* possibilities for how things can shake out in a square. But generally speaking, a "square" refers to a relationship system that involves four people. The members of a square aren't necessarily *all* involved with each other. In fact, it's quite rare that everyone is, since everyone in the square has to be attracted to one another and compatible for this to happen. No small order, especially if the square involves one or more heterosexual people.

Instead, like vees, most squares have hinge partners who link together people who aren't involved with one another.

People new to polyamory often think of these linked relationships as awkward and undesirable. However, polyamorous folks have a special word for our partner's other partner: *metamour.*

It's funny. Metamour relations are a form of improv — sometimes hilarious, sometimes awkward, sometimes painful, sometimes glorious, but never dull. Part of what makes it all so kooky is that we don't have scripts for how we're supposed to act towards our partner's other lover. We didn't see it modeled for us in Disney movies, and I can't remember ever reading about it in my favorite adolescent pleasure — *Sweet Valley High* books (oh the antics the Wakefield twins got up to!).

But here's the kicker – we actually had plenty of good models around us. They just weren't romantic.

You ever know someone who had two best friends? I sure did, and do.

Having a metamour is a lot like sharing a best friend.

You might go to make plans with them, and they're already going out with their other best friend. A lot of times? You're invited and can come, too. Other times it isn't something that can work out that way. And that's *okay*.

Just like a co-best friend, sometimes they'll become YOUR best friend, too, but sometimes it's a regular friendship…or maybe you can't stand them.

It's all okay.

If you can look at metamours as opportunities, something extra you're gaining (as a support to you, your partner, or both), instead of viewing shared time with your lover as something you're potentially losing? That's the key.

A study by Terri Conley and Amy Moors (2014) at the University of Michigan's Stigmatized Sexualities Lab found that polyamorous people tend to maintain more friendships as they keep a wider social network. They are also less likely to cut off contact after a break-up.[2]

Believe it or not, it's not just about the potential for kinky sex (although that certainly is nice if and when it happens). One of the best things about being polyamorous is the increased network of social supports, and metamours are a huge part of that.

Date on Your Own Instead of Dating as a Unit

The vast majority of couples new to polyamory approach it looking to date as a couple, and they typically search for a partner who will date them both together.

Transitioning to a polyamorous way of dating from a monogamous one can be a rather big adjustment.

But the way to most dramatically improve your chances of finding someone who will work with both of you?

It's to date on your own.

But wait! You might be thinking. *If we want someone to date us together, then why would we date on our own?*

There are a few different reasons. First off, it helps get rid of the power imbalance. *They're* dating on their own, after all, putting themselves out there. If you're dating on your own, you're doing that, too. Meeting them as a vulnerable person. Starting from a place of one on one rather than a place of two on one.

What's also interesting is that I've seen many successful triads form that started out as vee situations. A person was dating one member of a couple and through the process of getting to know them and then subsequently their metamour went on to find that a connection formed with the other half of the couple. Mind you, this doesn't *always* happen, but it's a lot more common than a couple successfully snagging a long-term triad with a package deal in place.

It's a funny thing, but the harder you push to be dated together as a couple, the less likely someone is going to want to date you both. It's human nature to rebel when we feel like someone is trying to force us to do something. In psychology, we call this principle *reactance* or *boomerang effect*. It's the reason why "reverse psychology" (i.e., the technique where we advocate for the thing opposite of what we want) is often such an effective persuasive technique. When a person tries too hard to convince us of something, we want to do the opposite.[3]

So date on your own. Have separate dating profiles. Be open about having an existing relationship but approach prospective partners with "I/me" rather than "we/us."

Don't Bait and Switch

However, when I say you need to date on your own, I mean it. You need to be comfortable if any given relationship doesn't evolve to something that involves both of you. You can absolutely be hopeful that a relationship might one day develop into something that involves multiple people you're seeing because it's great and wonderful when it works out that way, convenient time and harmony-wise, and potentially expands sexual possibilities depending on the cast of characters.

But no forcing it.

And whatever you do, no bait and switch.

I've seen this a lot with straight couples who send the woman out on a date by herself and then her male partner "conveniently" comes by partway through the date to join them.

Just. Don't.

It's dishonest to ambush a person on a date with unexpected guests. It'll come off as creepy and instantly undermine any trust that you've managed to build with them.

Seriously. It's one of the worst things you can do when you're dating polyamorous people.

Any attempts to date separately need to be honest and sincere. Otherwise, people will see right through them and they'll backfire.

Here are some tools to try when dating on your own:

- Wearing the friend hat

- Observing the good roommate standard

Wearing the Friend Hat

Part of what can feel daunting when trying to navigate polyamorous relationships is how few cultural models we have for a lot of what happens.

How are we supposed to act when we're sharing a romantic partner with others? And how should we interact with our metamours (i.e., our partner's other partners)?

Popular depictions of love triangles are *profoundly* unhelpful. Adversarial. A great how-to of what not to do. And we unfortunately don't have great examples of how we *should* act.

But as I mentioned before in the previous section "Consider a Square," we do have plenty of cultural models: They just aren't romantic.

We share friends with others all the time. Even our *best* friends sometimes will have a *second* best friend.

So one really helpful tool I have in my polyamory toolbox is the Friend Hat.

The Friend Hat is a really simple technique with a lot of uses. That's why it's one of my favorites.

When you're feeling a bit lost as to how to interact with a metamour, you can ask yourself:

> *What would I do if we weren't sharing a lover but a best friend?*

If you find yourself unhappy about your partner's choice in

other partners, the Friend Hat can be used as a self-check to differentiate between having practical concerns about a metamour and disliking them for other reasons:

> *Would I have concerns if a close friend were dating this person?*

You can also use the Friend Hat as a check to determine whether or not your partner is making reasonable requests.

> *Would what my partner is doing or asking for be appropriate if that same request came from a close friend?*

It also comes in handy to make sure you are doing the same.

> *Would what I'm asking from my partner be reasonable if I was asking this of a close friend?*

The Good Roommate Standard

Additionally, it can be a bit awkward at first dating other people separately when you live together. How are you supposed to work out a system of living with someone and sharing resources while dating other people separately?

Again, we can borrow a non-romantic example for managing this. Roommates run into the same issues that you'd be facing.

Here are some examples of the Good Roommate Standard in practice:

- If your date is cold, you can lend them a piece of your clothing, not your partner's.

- If you want to lend something to the new flame and it's your partner's, ask first. Drop it if they say no.

- If you mess up the kitchen cooking for a date, clean up after yourself. Don't expect your partner to do it.

Additionally, many couples who see others have rules about whether or not sex is allowed in the bed with the non-shared partner and under what circumstances.

Here are a few examples of common standards polyamorous people have established regarding this:

- No sex in the shared bed under any circumstances.

- Sex in the bed but strip the bed and wash the sheets immediately after.

- Sex in the bed is allowed but only on *your* side of the bed. If a guest sleeps over, you can surrender your side of the bed to them and sleep on your partner's side of the bed.

- Sex in the bed with others is permitted. No restrictions.

The key here is to have the conversation and find a consensus practice you can both agree to.

In addition, just like the old sock on the doorknob trick, many couples work out a system to prevent the random walk-in on amorous encounters.

Here are some example agreements:

- The other partner makes arrangements to stay out of the house for the entirety of the date (sometimes also playfully known as "sexile").

- A warning text is sent before the other partner returns home if their partner has a date at their shared home

- The person returning home during their partner's date makes a lot of noise as they're coming in.

- Sex only happens only in a certain room of the house or apartment, which means that the other partner can avoid barging in and may even be able to remain within the home and do other things while others are engaging in private time.

- The entire issue is sidestepped by having a "no sex in the house" rule.

- Sometimes a combination of multiple of these measures – quite commonly sexile for a period of time, a warning text, and then a very noisy reentrance into the home.

In any event, the Good Roommate Standard is a simple self-check:

Am I being a good roommate to my partner by doing this?

And a good check for others:

Is this behavior I'd tolerate from a roommate?

Now, don't get me wrong. Your partner isn't the *same thing* as a roommate. Seeing other people will not turn your sweetie into "just a roommate." In fact, the opposite tends to be true: Other partners have a way of thrumming up new relationship energy in existing relationships.

But the Good Roommate Standard can be really helpful for a simple reason: When you live with someone you love, you should treat them just as well (if not *better*) than you'd treat a roommate.

Lesson Ten

Building Personal Security

"Luminous beings are we...not this crude matter."

Yoda, Empire Strikes Back

If dating on your own sounds scary, ask yourself why.

A lot of people worry about feeling jealous or insecure. They're drawn to polyamory but nervous, feeling like they can only get a sense of emotional security by being in a monogamous relationship.

The good news is that it's possible to become emotionally secure in polyamorous relationships, even if you don't start out that way.

It's not instant, and it takes a lot of self-work, but with sustained practice, you can foster a sense of personal security.

Here are five steps to feeling more safe and secure in polyamorous relationships (and in general).

1. Acknowledge Your Feelings

The first step in conquering feelings of insecurity is acknowledging them. This is because getting rid of those feelings isn't the same as pretending you don't feel them in the first place. In fact, when people start to feel insecure, they often become ashamed of the insecurity, which starts a secondary trauma loop, where they're beating themselves up over and over again, punishing themselves for feeling (pretty normal) negative feelings. And beating yourself up and shaming yourself works against feeling secure.

Shame is the real killer. Not fear, anxiety, jealousy, insecurity. But shame. In basic survival terms, if the tribe rejects you, you die. Exile was death to our ancestors. Shame is a sense that you are unacceptable, that you don't belong. And your brain feels like it's life or death.

The worst part of all of this: Good people are especially prone to feeling bad about feeling bad.

It's not the feeling itself but our shame about the feeling – just like it's never the mistake that gets you, it's the cover-up.

While you can cover up those unacceptable feelings, by not sharing them, there's one person you'll never hide them from: Yourself.

So avoid covering up your feelings and make sure you acknowledge them.

2. But Don't Jump to Conclusions!

However, acknowledging feelings of insecurity isn't the same thing as trusting your emotions completely. Or saying that our fears are going to come true.

Our emotional systems have evolved to make snap judgments. To quickly identify threats and differentiate predator from prey. For that purpose, fear responses are perfectly well suited. But what protects us in the wild from getting eaten? Well, it doesn't work so well for modern relationships, which are less life and death and much more full of nuance.

> *"You cannot make yourself feel something you do not feel, but you can make yourself do right in spite of your feelings."*
>
> *Pearl Buck*

So even though you might feel worried, don't assume that your world is actually ending. And just because you feel bad, it also doesn't mean that anybody did anything wrong (though it could).

Rather than lashing out or doing something you regret, take a second to breathe and dig a little deeper into those feelings.

3. When You Feel Bad About Something, Ask Yourself "Why?"

Let's say you felt bad when you saw your partner flirting with another person. Why is that? What is that feeling telling you?

It can be uncomfortable to sit in this place, but do it as much as you can. Follow your fear to its logical conclusion.

Are you worried about getting replaced? Abandoned?

Part of what makes fear so powerful is that it's irrational and thrives in secrecy, and it's by dragging fear's arguments into the light of day and forcing fear to defend itself that we start to rob it of its power.

Sometimes, our fears are justified. Every now and then, there is a logical, well-founded basis to our fear. However, the vast majority of the time, fear overstates its case. Besides, in cases where our fears *are* justified, it's better to be in touch with that and act according to that reality. It's as Carl Sagan once said: "It is far better to grasp the universe as it really is than to persist in delusion, however satisfying and reassuring."

4. Identify and Question the Underlying Assumptions

Once you know what your fear is telling you, look for any underlying assumptions that it's making.

Folks who are new to polyamory frequently worry about a new partner outperforming them sexually. The underlying assumption here is that people select partners solely based on their sexual prowess. In situations like these, I've found it helpful to ask myself: What are other reasons that a partner could find value from being with me? What are some signs that my relationship is actually going well?

I also find it helpful to compare my assumptions about others to how I actually feel, think, and act. I struggled for a long time with the idea that sex was some sort of competition with runners-up facing the risk of being replaced — until I realized that's not how *I* view or treat people. And because it's not a view that I support or respect very much, I realized that if someone does view or treat people this way, they're fundamentally incompatible with me. Therefore, someone who would replace me in this way is someone *I don't actually want to be with.*

Depending on your specific concerns, the exact process and how you work through it will be different. What's important is thinking through your reactions and testing them against reality.

5. Remember: When It Comes to Feeling Secure, the Secret Ingredient Is Time

I think we've all been there. Sitting there, struggling over a particularly difficult problem. Pulling out our hair. Asking ourselves *What the HELL are we going to do about this?*

It feels like we're making absolutely no progress. Frustrated, we stop what we're doing and take a break. Do something else, even goof off for a while.

After a bit of time away, we revisit the problem…and immediately feel stupid. Of COURSE. It was so OBVIOUS. How did we not see this the first time?

This phenomenon, getting past a mental block when we revisit a problem after taking a break from it? It's well documented in psychology.

It's called incubation effect.

For me, building up my sense of personal security followed this kind of timeline. Practiced and practiced. I felt like I was making no progress. And then one day? I made a ton. Out of the blue. Kind of like the loading bar on your computer that sits at 10% for hours and then zips up the last 90% while you're looking away for two seconds.

So don't despair if you don't feel secure overnight. Keep digging. Keep analyzing. And keep on braving uncertainty. The only way past the discomfort is through it.

As Pamela Madsen writes in *Shameless*[4]:

> I don't think that staying with discomfort comes naturally. And finding ways to be with your discomfort is an essential skill for staying in the race. Any personal growth usually involves some kind of ability to stay with feelings of discomfort.
>
> Let's face it. If you are a seeker of any kind you will push boundaries. When we reach for personal transformation and start pushing edges and boundaries in our lives — we meet "the big work" and feelings of discomfort and wanting to flee from change surface.

Challenge the Underlying Assumptions of Toxic Monogamy

You're not alone. Transitioning from a monogamous way of thinking to a polyamorous one? Well, it can be quite an adjustment.

You might blame yourself for this difficulty, or you might blame polyamory. In reality, it's neither of these things.

The problem lies with toxic monogamy culture.

What is toxic monogamy culture? It's a set of societal beliefs that teach us that monogamy is the only ethical and healthy way to do relationships. Toxic monogamy does this in a way that's not only damaging to non-monogamy but to having healthy relationships of any sort, whether they're monogamous or polyamorous. It's basically the worst.

To be clear: Not all monogamy is toxic, and not all aspects of monogamy are toxic.

Monogamy in and of itself has so many good qualities. Sexual exclusivity in particular has a large upside. When practiced perfectly (although not always the case, even when it's meant to be), monogamy carries a lower STI risk. Though I've been polyamorous for quite some time, I could easily be sexually monogamous, if I could still have emotional connections with more than one person.

However, many people in long-term monogamous relationships become emotionally and socially isolated in a profound way. This is because a number of socially connected behaviors are perceived as infidelities. Toxic monogamy culturally trains us to be on high alert to detect cheating in our own relationships and the ones of those around us. This makes us overly sensitive to prosocial acts that could signal something insidious lurking beneath the surface.

For example, I recall a conversation I overheard between people who agreed that posting pictures with members of the opposite sex on Facebook was in fact cheating on your significant other. Even setting aside the fact that I'm not straight, this idea perplexed me.

As Noah Brand writes[5]:

> Hegemonic heterosexuality is the model for straight relationships that carries as many damaging, ridiculous, impossible assumptions and requirements as does hegemonic masculinity. Shall we list a few?
>
> Relationships are about finding The One you'll spend the rest of your life with. Naturally, a jealous and possessive form of monogamy is a strict requirement. It is necessary to hate all of one's exes, because they were not The One, and one must also be jealous of all one's partner's exes, because they touched your property before you even got there.

Given all this, it's not that adjusting to polyamory is impossible. Rather, it's that when left unchecked and unchallenged that the beliefs that accompany toxic monogamy will consistently torture a person in a polyamorous environment.

To combat this, challenge the underlying assumptions of toxic monogamy:

- Affection is zero sum. When you care for someone, that leaves less caring to give to others.
- One person *must* meet every possible emotional and social need that we have.
- We must do whatever is needed to protect The Relationship — a simultaneously fragile and all-important entity. If this involves complete isolation, then so be it.
- If a love is true and valid, we will never, ever be attracted to anyone else. Ever.

- If the intensity of that love changes, there is something wrong.

- If we are attracted to someone else, this means that our love isn't true. Or we're a horrible person. Or both. Probably both.

Even long-time polyamorous folks can struggle with some of this. These beliefs linger as nagging doubts. Even though we have actively rejected monogamy as a relationship style, we were raised in the same world. Toxic monogamy was modeled for us over and over again (through media, the relationships of others, etc.).

But it's important to realize that affection *isn't* zero sum. We don't care less for one person because we care for another. It sounds absurd to suggest that people who have more children love each child less than those who have fewer, but somehow when we say this of romantic love, a lot of people believe it.

I'll tell you, as a person with experience of being in multiple loving relationships at once, it just doesn't work that way: You can absolutely love more than one person at a time. Deeply. Differently.

Whether you're polyamorous, monogamous, or somewhere in between, one thing is true: Toxic monogamy culture is terrible for you.

Counter to what one might think, acting as though love is scarce is an easy way to lose it. Worrying you'll lose someone can drive them away. At the very least it can drive a wedge between you.

Lesson Eleven

Proper Care and Feeding of Unicorns:
How to Keep a Triad Healthy and Strong

"You have to believe. Otherwise, it will never happen."
Neil Gaiman, Stardust

So you've managed to find a compatible third partner and have formed a three-person relationship. Congratulations!

You've gotten further than most couples who set out to find a unicorn.

Guess that's it, right? You all live happily ever after. Riding off into the sunset and all that jazz.

Maybe. And if it works out, effortlessly, naturally, awesome.

But sometimes it can be a little tricky knowing how to maintain your new relationship. What to do. What to avoid.

So before you go, I'd like to share some advice on that, gleaned from my own experiences and those of the happy, long-lasting triads that I have known.

- Invest in Every Pairing in the Triad

- Don't Assume, Communicate

  - Start with Small Things

  - Let Go of Yes, Learn to Say No

  - What Is That Thing You Are Scared to Say?

  - Boundary Setting 101

- Self-Care (for Everyone)

- Inclusive Is Good, Limit Exclusivity

Invest in Every Pairing in the Triad

Earlier in the book, in the section on triads vs. vees, I explained that in a triad there are basically four different relationships:

1. Alex and Baley

2. Alex and Codi

3. Baley and Codi

4. Alex, Baley, and Codi

One stumbling block that newly polyamorous couples encounter is that they expect to be going from one relationship to two! That's hard enough, doubling your work. However, in actuality, you're going from one relationship to *four*.

This is daunting but certainly doable.

The *key* to doing this and doing it well is to make sure that you invest in *every* pairing in the triad. Don't neglect any one of these four dynamics, especially the first three.

Understand that Your Relationship Is Going to Change

"I'm worried I'll never be able to look at them in the same way."

I hear this often from people who are polycurious but nervous about taking the leap and opening up.

I'll be honest. I have never seen a situation where a couple opened up and their relationship *didn't* change. However, mmany times, it changed for the better.

After they got out of the woods and got past the rough parts, they really began to see each other again. They saw each other with new eyes. They stopped taking each other for granted. They communicated much better, trusted each other a ton, and their sex life got amazing. Not that they even KNEW they had been taking each other for granted, mind you.

However, there's a concept in psychology called "habituation to a stimulus," and the principle translates well to long-term relationships. When a person is around in a relatively unchanging way, they don't stick out as much to you. New experiences and extra variables really have a way of making you notice each other again in vivid ways. It's really cool.

We fear change. It's a survival mechanism, wired deep in our brains. Change is perceived as threat, something that could obliterate us in an instant, drive us to extinction. While there can be unpleasant changes, ones that are true threats, the vast majority of changes we experience in our lives are neutral or positive. In fact, I would argue, that the biggest threat to survival in modern life (physical, emotional, and otherwise) is to be rigid, inflexible, and unwilling to adapt to circumstances.

But yes, many couples find that once they adjust, their preexisting relationship is stronger and more exciting.

Don't Assume, Communicate

Communication is incredibly important in all relationships but especially so in polyamorous ones. Really, no one should take things for granted, but it becomes even more inadvisable in alternative relationships where there are few cultural models to follow.

Building your relationship is a custom engineering project, and as architects, you need to communicate well in order to successfully collaborate. To design and manage this project.

What follows is not intended as an exhaustive guide to communication. Indeed, entire *libraries* have been devoted to how to successfully communicate. However, it's a start. I'll also list some resources that you can seek out in order to read more. Because being awesome at communication is a lifelong project, and the more you study (and practice), the better.

Here's a general guideline though: Say as much as needs to be said, and then once you've done that, say a little more. When in doubt, it's better to repeat yourself on occasion than to neglect to mention something important.

Be as direct as you possibly can in your communication. Do not beat around the bush and hope that someone catches on to the gist of what you mean and inquires further.

The process of moving from an indirect style to a direct style of expressing yourself can feel scary and at times completely overwhelming, but it's important work.

While being indirect can feel more comfortable (especially if we're used to it), indirect communication often fails when we have uncomfortable feelings or need something our partner isn't giving us, leading to passive-aggressive communication or relationship testing.

Start with Small Things

I'm a recovering people pleaser. When I first started being more direct with the people in my life, I felt like I was yelling at them.

At the time, I had gotten into the habit of just going along with things that didn't matter so much. This was harmless enough in isolation, but unfortunately, it had led to my staying quiet about big things, too, which predictably caused problems. So at a certain point, I had to stop defaulting to just letting things slide.

Breaking from that pattern was *hard*. A simple "You know, I'm not so into that idea," about something trivial like soda preference felt like I was about to create some kind of emotional avalanche. Think Ricola and the Swiss Alps but with a catastrophic ending.

But no, nobody died because I wanted a root beer.

And as I saw that I could let people know what I wanted and needed with the little stuff, I got better at expressing myself about things that mattered a lot more. The high-stakes conversations.

The skills I built by being direct about little things served me well when we needed to talk about big issues.

So test the waters first with small issues. Learn to swim before you jump into the deep end. You don't have to conquer every conversation on day one.

Let Go of Always Yes, Learn to Say No

I used to be terrified of telling people "no." Setting boundaries with people, although necessary, requires a lot of direct communication. And hardest for me at the time: Sometimes you have to tell people no!

It can be scary to say no to someone. You might hurt someone's feelings. They might get upset. Even angry.

However, what I had to learn was when we tell people no is when we really get to know them. People tend to act alike so long as you are saying yes to everything they want from you.

This meant that not only was I getting the benefits of the boundaries I set, I was also more easily able to differentiate between people who were reasonable and cared about me, those who were selfish and completely unwilling to compromise, and everyone else who fell somewhere in between.

What Is That Thing You Are Scared to Say?

When it comes to communication, I've learned to pay a different kind of attention to my fear. Rather than doing what the fear says (which is "don't tell them what you feel"), I look at where my fear is pointing. At what my fear wants to hide because it will leave me too vulnerable, too exposed. What I'm afraid people I love might judge me for. And instead of listening to fear's directive to stay in the shadows and keep it hidden, I say that thing that makes me vulnerable.

That's because the thing I'm scared to say is often the thing I most need to share with them.

It's little surprise that polyamorous folks have the mantra: "Communicate, communicate, communicate."

The word communication itself means "sharing." It comes from Latin: *communicatio*(n-), from the verb *communicare*, "to share."

Boundary Setting 101

Asserting boundaries is about establishing what you are or are not okay with. Setting appropriate boundaries is particularly important in achieving healthy relationships with others.

However, boundaries are *very* individual. They call them *personal* boundaries for a reason.

As a starting point here are some basic healthy boundaries to keep in mind:

- Not allowing others to manipulate or force you into doing things you don't want to do and not doing so to anyone else.

- Not tolerating others yelling at you or calling you names and not doing this to others.

- Not blaming others for things that are your responsibility and not tolerating inappropriate blaming from others.

- Understanding that your feelings are separate from another person's, although you certainly can have empathy for their situation.

- Being able to request space (physical, temporal, privacy, etc.) and allowing others to request the same from you.

To a lot of recovering people pleasers, setting these boundaries can seem daunting. Even controlling. But boundary setting is different from controlling people, which is about telling other people what to do. Especially when it has little or nothing to do with you.

Here are some simple boundary-setting statements:

- "I'm not willing to argue with you right now. I'd be happy to talk to you later when we're both calm."

- "I'm sorry, but I won't be doing that. I won't be loaning you any more money until you pay off what I loaned you before."

Whenever possible, use as non-blaming language as possible. Be firm, but not on the attack. Generally speaking, "I" statements come off as more diplomatic than "you" statements.

So rather than saying, "You're always snooping through my stuff," try saying:

"I feel violated when you look through my things. I need some privacy in a relationship. Otherwise, I feel like I'm under a magnifying glass. Please do not go through my things without asking."

Bear in mind that it's possible to use "I" statements in an aggressive or ineffective way. "I feel that you're always snooping through my stuff," or "I hate that you're always snooping through my stuff," are both blaming and ineffective.

While you might feel that blame is warranted, blaming others put them on the defensive, which makes them less likely to listen and accommodate your needs. Avoid blanket generalized statements including words like "always" and "never." These feel particularly unfair to a person receiving them. It's a rare person who does something always or never, and the exaggeration aspect undercuts the truth of what you're saying.

Instead, focus on your feelings.

When setting boundaries, it can be helpful to share the potential consequences of violating that boundary. However, be honest with yourself and your partners as you do.

Don't threaten things you aren't willing to follow through on. If you say you'll have to leave a relationship over a certain behavior, be prepared to do so. Reserve those consequences for the worst violations, especially after repeated violations with no efforts to improve.

Thankfully, proposed consequences need not be so dire. Using the last example about snooping, you might tell your partner that if they don't stop looking through your things, you will have to lock your things up or change your passwords on a computer.

If you find that the issue of invasion of your privacy is widespread and particularly troubling, causing you to feel disrespected in a way that harms your relationship, you might pursue counseling, or, as mentioned, there is always ending the relationship (just don't start there if you can help it).

If at all possible, it's best to discuss what your boundaries are *before* they're violated. I'm aware of most of mine due to past relationship experiences I've had. I find it goes more smoothly if you can preemptively share those with new partners. Not only are new partners less likely to violate those boundaries, but if they do? The resulting discussion usually entails less conflict and drama if it's not completely new information to them.

Suggested Further Reading on Communication

Crucial Conversations: Tools for Talking When Stakes Are High by Al Switzler, Joseph Grenny, Kerry Patterson, and Ron McMillan

Daring Greatly by Brené Brown

Where to Draw the Line by Anne Katherine

Self-Care (for Everyone)

Unhealthy self-sacrifice can happen in polyamorous relationships just as easily as in monogamous ones.

In fact, I think that polyamorous folks are at *higher* risk for neglecting important self-care (especially folks with caretaker personalities). There's a lot of societal pressure, especially for women, to sacrifice yourself to take care of others.

Even women who don't have children are expected to put romantic partners first, and the cultural mythos goes that if you love someone enough, there are very few sacrifices that are too much.

I experienced this firsthand when I was polysaturated (arguably oversaturated). The relationship that suffered the most was the one with myself. I had no free time.

Self-care and exactly what that can entail can look very different to each person.

However, the basic difference between setting self-care as low priority or high priority is this:

Low self-care priority: Once I've taken care of every other important person and task in my life, then I'll start taking care of myself.

High self-care priority: I will take care of myself, and then I can take better care of every other person and task in my life.

Self-care can *feel* selfish, especially if you're used to putting yourself last, but in practice, we are best able to help other people when we're in good shape (emotionally, physically, and otherwise), which involves taking good care of ourselves.

Keep in mind that self-care isn't just important for you, the members of the couple. Your third partner also needs to practice self-care. Sometimes this might mean that you're inconvenienced by your other partner prioritizing taking care of themselves. Deal gracefully with that inconvenience.

Supporting your partner isn't always just about being there for them when they need you. It's also about giving them the time and space to focus on themselves when they need it.

Inclusive is Good, Limit Exclusivity

Since your relationship started first, it's likely you'll have many shared memories that your third partner wasn't a part of.

You *can* reminisce. You can talk about the time the two of you were plastered on Christmas Day in Niagara Falls (mmmm Tim Horton's and screwdrivers, amirite? Good times), but if you do, you might want to show your third partner some photos and then segue into fun stuff you'd like to do with them. Maybe even suggest a return trip with the three of you and how that would be even more fun.

Additionally, be careful with "private jokes" between you as a couple. Don't let these existing in-jokes make your third partner feel excluded. Explain them and create new ones that include all three of you.

Be on the lookout for things that could potentially make them feel left out. Don't make a big kerfuffle about it, mind you, but do your best to pull them in and make them feel included. Whenever possible, strive to create new inclusive memories as a triad.

Because the last thing you want is your third partner feeling like they're standing outside on the sidewalk, cold and hungry, watching people in a restaurant eat their fancy, fancy dinners.

Conclusion

Go Forth and Love!

"I am a leaf on the wind, watch how I soar."

Wash, Serenity

The bottom line of all this advice is to be as open, fair, and ethical as you can.

This isn't *just* because treating people we date well is the right thing to do (though it is), it's also the most surefire way I've encountered to attract good partners.

So if you can't treat others well for high-minded moral reasons, consider that it has purely self-serving potential as well. If you want people to be good to you, you should be good to them.

"But wait a second," you might be saying. "Can altruism be adopted for selfish means? Can you become a giving person to be a bigger hit with lovers? Or does the selfishness of the reasons for adopting it make it no longer altruistic?"

Researcher Daniel Batson[6] has given a lot of thought and attention to these sorts of questions.

As Batson writes: "Especially in so value-laden an area as our helping of others, we cannot assume we know — or if we know that we will report — our true motives."

In his work Batson has focused on whether or not altruism actually exists and if seemingly selfless acts instead have hidden selfish upsides:

> If a friend's distress caused you distress, and you stayed up all night providing comfort in order to reduce your own distress, then your motivation was egoistic. True, you sought to make your friend feel better, but that was not your ultimate goal. It was only instrumental in allowing you to reach the ultimate goal of feeling better yourself.

> If your friend's distress caused you distress, but you helped in order to relieve the friend's distress as an end in itself, then your motivation was altruistic. True, by relieving the friend's distress you probably relieved your own distress and avoiding feeling guilty. Yet, to the extent that these outcomes were not your ultimate goal but only unintended consequences of pursuing the ultimate goal of relieving the friend's distress, your motivation was altruistic.

Batson argues that the secret ingredient in all of this is empathy. Regardless of any other factors, if we feel empathy towards another person, we will help them even if it has no upside for us. In the absence of empathy, a complex social calculus takes place in which we will help if there's an upside for us (even if it's not readily apparent to others and maybe even hidden from ourselves).

And I'm willing to bet that empathy is the secret sauce to differentiate between "Nice Guys" (that trusty old Internet meme) who expect to be rewarded with sex when they're halfway decent to women in short intervals and actual altruistic dudes (and dudettes, people, etc.) who are giving, understand, and yes, hot.

Actually caring about other people.

It makes a big difference.

So do your best to remember other people's needs. Care about them and take actions that demonstrate this caring.

Wanting to treat people well puts you halfway there.

Because in the words of the Kurt Vonnegut, "We are what we pretend to be, so we must be careful about what we pretend to be."

Don't Be Unicorn Hunters, Be Unicorn Ranchers

It all comes down to one simple fact: Couples really shouldn't be hunting unicorns.

Instead, couples should be unicorn ranchers. If we want unicorns to come and visit us, we should create a safe place for them.

If you want a unicorn, you must first create a unicorn sanctuary. Grow grass, plant flowers. Tend it. Leave the gate open. But don't set any traps.

Make sure your relationship is in order. "Relationship broken, add more people" never works. A unicorn isn't going to be your big fluffy life raft. They are a person with wants and needs of their own, ones that don't revolve around your preexisting relationship.

Don't hunt them down. Don't conquer them. And when they show up, of their own accord, in this magical refuge you have created, whatever you do, don't fence them in. Feed your unicorn.

If they like you, if they trust you, they'll stay.

Being a unicorn is fantastic, yet terrifying. You're universally pursued, but you never know whether it's because someone wants to cut off your horn, kill you and mount your head on the wall, or keep you at their ranch and spoil you.

If you're looking for a unicorn, as many are, don't be the hunting kind. Be the spoiling kind. Be unicorn ranchers.

Appendix A

Sample Relationship Agreements

Here are three sample agreements from some polyamorous people that they report work very well for their respective relationships. This is not an exhaustive listing. As you look over these, you'll likely note that they're very different from one another. Relationship agreements are very individual, and yours will likely look different from any of the ones listed here.

Sample Agreement 1

Notification is required for the following:

- Crushes or serious romantic interest in someone else

- A date with someone new, before it happens

Sexual activity:

- The expected maximum level of physical intimacy during any given date will be disclosed, understanding that less can happen based on the other person's comfort level, but that things should not progress beyond that agreed-upon point.

- At the time that this expectation is disclosed, our existing partner's comfort level will be taken into account. If one of us is uncomfortable, the allowed level of physical intimacy may be adjusted to a less serious level.

- If things seem to be progressing beyond that agreed-upon comfort point on any given date, we must text our partner about it and clear the more serious activity with them. If the partner doesn't respond to the text or doesn't approve the more serious act, physical activity is not to proceed beyond the point agreed upon previously.

- In terms of sexual activity, we define the following activities as going from least serious to most serious: closed mouth kissing, open mouth kissing, clothed fondling/groping, unclothed fondling/groping, oral sex (as either giver or recipient), vaginal sex, anal sex.

- We will be tested every 6 months for the full panel available at our local Planned Parenthood, as will any new partners prior to oral, vaginal, or anal intercourse. Those results will be made available to us and others in paper and/or electronic form.

- Condoms will be worn for all vaginal or anal intercourse with new partners.

- Failure to maintain these standards of sexual safety will result in no sexual activity between us until a 6-month interval elapses and a proper STI baseline can be reestablished.

Miscellaneous:

- No sex in our bed. Clothes-on cuddling is okay in the bed with others.

- All dates should be logged in the shared Google Calendar with that person's name as well as an accurate timeframe for the date. If the date involves staying at someone else's house, the entry should include an address and phone number as well so that the other partner can call if there's an emergency or a safety concern. In some circumstances, being connected with this person via instant messenger or text can suffice for contact info, if all parties agree.

Sample Agreement 2

General:

- We do not object to things on emotional grounds. When we are making decisions regarding other partners, we consider the logical outcomes of our actions and not their emotional impact.

- Don't get anyone sick, jailed, or pregnant.

- Have fun.

Sexual activity:

No permission or notification is required for any of the following:

- Kissing

- Making out

- Dry humping

- Dirty talking/flirting/phone sex

- Low-risk BDSM activities (flogging, spanking, etc.)

- Hand jobs (but please wash hands and thoroughly inspect for cuts first, and if in doubt wear gloves)

- Toy play (vibrators, strap ons, etc.)

Preexisting partners *must* be consulted before any of the following:

- Oral sex (giving or receiving)

- Vaginal sex

- Anal sex

- Higher-risk BDSM activities (blood play, anything involving oral, anal, or vaginal sex, etc.)

Up-to-date testing for HIV, chlamydia, gonorrhea, and syphilis must be received for prospective partners in these areas prior to consultation with preexisting partners.

Preexisting partners will have the opportunity to deny the request for these higher-risk acts based on acceptable risk factors — whether these are due to STI results, personal characteristics, or past behavior of the candidate.

Miscellaneous:

- Do NOT cancel preexisting dates to schedule a date with someone else. This is disruptive and causes scheduling problems.

Sample Agreement 3

General:

- We only date people together. One-on-one dates can happen in the early stages of meeting someone, but the ultimate goal is to find someone we can date together.

- Nothing sexual happens (even kissing) without both of us being there, except as in "alone time," defined below in "Permission."

Permission:

Permission must be obtained prior to any of the following:

- Going on a date with someone new

- Kissing

- Any other sexual activities

- Alone time with a partner that we are dating together (for the first time and each subsequent time that it occurs until we mutually agree that it is okay as a standing rule)

- Calling the new partner by any relationship label (boyfriend, girlfriend, etc.)

Any and all dating messages sent to others will be reviewed by the other partner and approved prior to sending to new dating prospects. This right may be waived with the consent of the reviewing partner.

Hierarchy:

- We are primary to one another, and our existing relationship comes first.

- We are given higher priority when it comes to scheduling with one another.

- Plans with secondary partners will be rescheduled (and without any complaining) to accommodate plans that we have made with each other.

- If anything makes one of us jealous, we can request for it to stop, and that request will be honored.

- If one of us doesn't think a new person is a good dating prospect for any reason, the relationship will not happen. We must both approve of them.

Miscellaneous:

- You must never in any online dating communication fail to disclose the fact that you are already in a relationship, even in the beginning stages.

- No overnight dates that result in one of us sleeping alone. Even if alone time is approved, you must return home by 3 am.

- No phone sex or cybersex.

- No sending anyone nudes.

- Don't call others by our pet names for one another.

Appendix B

Opening Your Existing Relationship: A Checklist

What are your...

Motivations

- Why do you want to do this?

- What are you hoping to get out of the experience? People have a variety of reasons why they open relationships.

- What values are important to you when it comes to relationships?

- What role do those play in your current relationship?

- How do you ideally see them playing out in new relationships? Generally speaking, of course, since new partners will bring their own values as well.

- What does "Relationship" and "Love" and "Sex" mean to each of you? (You might be surprised!)

Starting Out

- How actively will you seek out partners?

- How much freedom or autonomy do we need?

- Will you make online dating profiles? Separately or Together?

- Will you seek out polyamory groups, kink groups, or swinging clubs—or go it alone?

- Is one partner in charge of seeking? Are you only going as a complete unit, or will you date separately?

Relationship Agreements

- What painful scenarios have you run into in the past (while monogamous, casually non-monogamous, or polyamorous) that you are looking to avoid?

- Are there any measures that you can implement to prevent these?

- Do you want to have a permission structure (i.e., to have a standard that you ask and obtain approval from an existing partner before we start a new relationship) or a notification structure (i.e., don't need permission but should tell your partners things happened after they happen)? Or something else altogether (e.g., don't ask don't tell, etc.)?

- What are the consequences of breaking the relationship agreement?

- How often will you revisit the agreement?

- Do you have an "out clause"?

- Is one party able to unilaterally end things at any one time?

- Do you have veto power over your partner's other relationships? And if you do, what does that look like?

Logistics

- What concerns you regarding sexual safety?

- What STI testing and safe-sex practices do you require?

- What are the consequences of breaking safer-sex practices?

- How will you pay for dates? (If one partner isn't earning money, this can lead to issues.)

- If there are children, how will you deal with child care?

Emotions – In the Deep of It

- What happens when a partner starts to feel in love?

- Do you understand the differences between New Relationship Energy (NRE), Old Relationship Energy (ORE), Eros/Lust, Friendship, etc.?

- Are you allowed to become emotionally invested?

- What happens when one falls in love, and the other does not?

- How will you react if one partner gets hurt by someone you're dating?

Helpful Hints

Date separately. Trying to date as a single unit tends to overwhelm and intimidate (and can be a bit icky), but don't bait and switch!

Glossary

Descriptive Hierarchy

    A style of hierarchical polyamory in which certain relationships are considered higher priority than others but only for the time being. In a descriptive hierarchy, future dynamics are not dictated. Labels used are only describing the current state of the hierarchy, usually based on things like level of entanglement, length of relationships, etc.

Dyad

    Another term for couple, or a pair of romantic partners

Hierarchical Polyamory

    A style of polyamory in which certain relationships are considered higher priority than others. This is usually noted by calling some relationships "primary" and others "secondary." Can take the form of descriptive or prescriptive hierarchy.

Hinge

    A person having relationships with two (or more) partners who aren't romantically involved with one another

Metamour

    A partner's other partner

New Relationship Energy (aka NRE)

    A mental and emotional state experienced at the beginning of romantic and sexual relationships. Also known as limerence.

Non-Hierarchical Polyamory

A style of polyamory in which no relationship is ranked or put before the other. There are no primaries or secondaries (or tertiaries).

Old Relationship Energy (aka ORE)

The dynamic of a long-standing established romantic or sexual relationship. Related to the Greek concept of *pragma* or mature love. Also known as companionate love.

Open Polyamory

A style of polyamory in which relationships are open to new partners

Polyfidelity

A style of polyamory in which multiple people are committed to one another and are not open to new partners

Polyamory

The practice of participating simultaneously in more than one serious romantic or sexual relationship with the knowledge and consent of all partners

Polysaturated

A state in which a polyamorous person is dating enough people that they couldn't manage more relationships even if they wanted to

Prescriptive Hierarchy

A style of hierarchical polyamory in which certain relationships are designated higher priority than others with the understanding that they always will be

Primary Relationship

A relationship that is prioritized over others and/or one that involves significant entanglement, e.g., living together, sharing finances, raising children, seeing each other frequently, etc. Other terms that are commonly used include anchor partner or nesting partner.
Note: Polyamorous people can have multiple primary relationships.

Relationship Escalator

A widely held cultural belief about relationships that they must follow a particular pattern, leading to progressively more serious commitment

Secondary Relationship

A relationship that is considered generally lower priority than a primary relationship and/or one that is lower entanglement

Sexile

A portmanteau for "sexual exile." When one partner stays out of the shared dwelling when they know their partner has a date at the house, in order to give them some privacy.

Solo Polyamory (aka solo poly)

A category of polyamory that covers a wide range of relationships that take a "free agent" approach to poly. Many solo polyamorists don't choose to share a home or finances with intimate partners generally tend to emphasize themselves as individuals and not part of a couple or triad.

Square

A relationship system that refers to four people, most commonly two couples

Tertiary Relationship

A relationship where partners see each other infrequently. Very low entanglement. These are also sometimes known as comet relationships.

Throuple

A three-person couple. *See also: Triad*

Triad

A group of three people who are all romantically involved with one another in some way (less commonly also known as a throuple)

Unicorn

Polyamorous, bisexual person (usually a woman) who will date both members of a couple

Unicorn Hunter

A couple (especially a heterosexual one) who opens up their relationship looking to date a unicorn together

Vee

A type of relationship involving three people in which two of the members share a partner in common but aren't involved with one another. Gets its name from the letter V. The shared partner is commonly called a hinge.

Veto Power

The ability to unilaterally end the relationship your partner is having with someone else

References and Recommended Reading

End Notes / References

1. Dawn M. v. Michael M., 55 Misc 3d 865, (Sup. Ct. Suffolk County, 2017)

2. Conley, T. D., & Moors, A. C. (2014). More oxygen please!: How polyamorous relationship strategies might oxygenate marriage. Psychological Inquiry, 25, 56-63.

3. Mann, M. F., & Hill, T. (1984). Persuasive communications and the boomerang effect: Some limiting conditions to the effectiveness of positive influence attempts. Advances in Consumer Research, 11, 66-70.

4. Madsen, P. (2011). Shameless: How I ditched the diet, got naked, found true pleasure…and somehow got home in time to cook dinner. Emmaus, PA: Rodale.

5. Brand, N. (2012, March 13). Hegemonic heterosexuality. Retrieved March 21, 2017, from https://goodmenproject.com/sex-relationships/hegemonic-heterosexuality/

6. Batson, C. D. (2016). The altruism question: Toward a social-psychological answer. New York, NY: Routledge.

Additional Reading

Crucial Conversations:
Tools for Talking When Stakes Are High
Al Switzler, Joseph Grenny, Kerry Patterson, and Ron McMillan

Daring Greatly
Brené Brown

Where to Draw the Line
Anne Katherine

Stepping off the Relationship Escalator
Amy Gahran

Sex at Dawn
Cacilda Jethá

The Ethical Slut
Dossie Easton and Janet Hardy

Learn more at

https://poly.land

and

https://braided.studio

About the Author

Page Turner

Page Turner doesn't believe in unicorns; they believe in her.

An award-winning author, poet, and playwright, Page works as a relationship coach in the poly and kink communities. With a professional background in psychological research and organizational behavioral consulting, Page is best described as a "total nerd."

She lives in the Cleveland suburbs where she tells bad jokes and drinks good wine with the people she loves.

Also by Page Turner

Poly Land: My Brutally Honest Adventures in Polyamory

Available on Amazon and most online book sellers.

Made in the USA
Monee, IL
02 March 2020

22592465R00059